COMEDY

AND OTHER OBSERVATIONS

Howard Winn

Copyright© 2020 Howard Winn
ISBN: 978-93-90202-83-6

First Edition: 2020
Rs. 200/-

Cyberwit.net
HIG 45 Kaushambi Kunj, Kalindipuram
Allahabad - 211011 (U.P.) India
http://www.cyberwit.net
Tel: +(91) 9415091004 +(91) (532) 2552257
E-mail: info@cyberwit.net

Printed at Repro India Limited.

CONTENTS

REALITY SHOW

I find no meaning in popular works about
zombies, human vampires, or extraterrestrial aliens,
nor even the legendary Texan chupacabra –
blood-sucker human flesh eating
monsters of the myths, ancient
and contemporary, even when written
by well-known authors to pander,
or to make the New York Times Best Seller List,
and pay for their next European tour,
not when
we have our very own investment bankers,
our hedge-funders, pyramid schemes,
insider trading, cold-calling predators,
off-shore tax havens, numbered bank accounts,
money-laundering, oligarchs, Russian
and other wise, bought elections
that subvert democracy to boot.
Reality is quite sufficient,
enough to raise the hairs on the back of the neck
in dread and distress.

BELIEVER

He trusts in absolutes
because without them
he feels as if he were
walking on ice,
and could slip to his knees
with broken bones,
or break through into
unknown depths and
drown in the uncertain
deepness of skepticism
where ancient sea monsters
may swim, or not.

CONTAMINATED

Men in space suits are removing
lead and asbestos
from a house down the street.
Begun in the twenties,
this house remained from when innocence
prevailed as did cancer the crab,
moving sideways into the lungs
and other vital organs, both male and female,
from room paint, hot air ducts and shingles
covering innocent Cape Cod cottages,
moon walkers in airtight costumes
earn a healthy living from the fear of death,
this summer house is now year round.
It holds an angular blonde mother
who runs along Shore Road with like wives,
a sinewy square-jawed father who drives
his hefty SUV to work and to his health club,
and coaches his vigorous son for little league fame
in the weekly mowed large side lawn
cared for by a landscape service that comes
in substantial truck and trailer to haul away
the unwanted grass.
across the street from our front windows.
In the mist of life, death by carcinogens lurks
in the up-scale décor and in the pipes of necessity.
Running, running, running,
they cannot run away.
Running, running, running,
they cannot run away.
Nes est certain, vita est non

THE LONELINESS OF THE GROCERY CART

Abandoned in the parking lot,
the solitary shopping cart,
untended, rests alone against
the sign that reserves the space
for the handicapped
or the parent with a small child.
Are they comparable?
Someone who does not
move easily in the world,
or is encumbered by infant,
has struggled into a vehicle,
one must presume,
leaving this empty wheeled basket behind,
shirking an obligation of society
to follow directions,
Rather than push it to
the corral for carts,
where the others properly placed
wait for the red-shirted
attendant to tug a train of carts,
like a small child
with a line of wooden toys,
back to the store.
Someone has abandoned it
Do we find meaning
in the loneliness of that shopping cart?

GHOSTLY

In the woods behind the house,
or in the driveway curving down
to dark spaces under Hemlocks,
I sometimes catch a hint of cigar
smoke on the cool air.
It is there and then it is not,
blown away into evergreen trees.
My father, smoker, has been dead
over a decade.
Shadows moving behind thin curtains
have the shape of my mother,
bent in that question mark of spine
that seems the fate of English genes,
but now it is a stranger in the room.
She has been under a bronze tablet
laid in green grass at the Rural Cemetery
for eight years less than her husband.
The shades of friends crowd the audience
at concerts and plays, milling amongst
the living: even at work ghosts slip between
desks and out of doors just at the edge
of my vision. There is a dim line between times,
faint and giddy as it slips to left or right
without warning. We catch the odors
and the shapes on the edge before they
slip back across the river.
There were no apparitions of this kind
for my youth. Demons wavered
then in faint outline to my naive eyes,

but darkened hallways, unlit cellars,
blank closets are empty now.
This present ghost, neither friendly
nor unfriendly, is a gathering of age.

WHEN THE POET DIES
(IN MEMORY OF SEAMUS HEANEY)

his voice is heard,
rising to the top of the Irish stew,
seasoning still swirling
as the cooking goes on.
The onions, mushrooms, and meat
of his art mixes with
the potatoes and broth
of his imagination.
As in the fairy tale,
this meal is never-ending
and the pot cannot be emptied.
Some will dine from this
poetic vessel, and some
will look for the passing
moment's fast food at the strip mall
of the mind instead,
having no taste for gourmet
thinking.

CARDS OF IDENTIFICATION

I was standing in the supermarket aisle,
blue and white corn chips on my right,
flavored, non-caloric seltzer
and pure Maine spring water on my left,
when an elderly woman called out,
"Oh, Mr. Kramer! Mr. Kramer!"
an unfamiliar name, in my direction.
I looked beyond us, in the point of the compass
she was facing, down the aisle.
She, her husband pushing a laden cart –
the most prominent product being
a twenty-four roll package of toilet paper
balanced on bread, cold-cuts, vegetables,
milk, cottage cheese, eggs, bananas —
and I were its sole inhabitants.
They came up to me, beaming recognition
and welcome on two wrinkled faces.
She smelled of cinnamon, he of tobacco.
"We're your neighbors," she said. "The Longmans."
"Are you still walking? How old are you now?"
I suppose I should have said, "I think
you have mistaken me for someone else,"
and then, perhaps, "All white-bearded men
can look remarkably alike,"
but I did not, for a reason I cannot fathom.
Perhaps so as not to disappoint their eagerness,
as endearing as that of a small child
upon observing a puppy.

Instead, I answered, "Oh, yes. One has to keep active."
Then, "Old enough," I laughed,
because they seemed so to need a genuine ancient here.
"Well, God bless," she said.
"Happy Holidays," he said.
"The same to you," I said, and we all smiled
and parted beneath the plastic ropes of fake holly
and to the late Bing Crosby singing
about his perfect white Christmas.
We nodded again in the parking lot
as we rolled carts to cars, and that was that.
Now, the question is –
have I become in some way a Mr. Kramer?

Am I still me? Has nothing changed?

Will I ever see these self-identified neighbors again?
And where _is_ their neighborhood?

Good luck, Mr. Kramer, wherever you are,

when you and this couple meet again.

INNER SPACE

Stephen Hawking,
tied to his wheel chair and his talking computer,
would like to fly weightless
just below outer space
for one short trip.
Outliving Lou Gehrig,
trapped in that immobile body
but with children
and grandchildren,
he is not tranquil in the head.
He would soar in the arc,
courtesy of Zero Gravity Corporation,
a profitable private company,
he insists, with his medical team,
and feel the heaviness of heightened gravity
alternate with the euphoric lightness
of being freed from the force guiding Newton's apple.
Humans will have to flee this earth
in some future time,
he states in his metallic machine voice,
when it will become uninhabitable,
as he says it inevitably will,
for his and our descendants,
and he, ever the intrepid experimenter,
would test the possibilities
insofar as he is able.

GRANDDAUGHTER

(For Emma)

Dancing on the beach,
embraced by a kite nearly as tall as she,
her skirt flaps in the wind
like a flag.
She whirls and flings
the kite skyward
where invisible air
as solid as the sea
lifts it over her.
Hovering on the fluid edge of childhood,
like the shifting spindrift
line of the cove's sandy rim
retreating and advancing,
she tugs back on kite string
tying the fabric to earth
as it seeks escape.
Escape and connection
gives it the power to fly.
When she crosses the thresh-hold
she will understand that paradox.
Now it is just play.

BUTTON COLLECTION

Bringing order to our mother's house,
as she sat in her rocking chair
watching a daytime television program,
my sister threw out old candy boxes
containing buttons hoarded
from at least sixty years.
They sounded like shaken gourds
as they went into the trash;
although not in Caribbean rhythm.
Snipped from worn clothes
in a mild fever of saving,
these buttons were of all sizes,
shapes and colors, buttoning down
the past even when occasionally
reused in the present.
They might come in handy,
my mother used to say,
and waste not want not.
I think that she just loved
the myriad colors, shapes,
the quantities, the weight ,
the implicit histories,
the textures of enclosure.

FRONT YARD PEOPLE

Grass is carefully shorn,
flowers ring the dogwood
and line the walk.
Leaves are plucked from the perfect
lawn as soon as they fall.
Dandelions are forbidden.
The walk is swept clean
as it leads to the front door.
It is a picture of perfection
in the front yard.
Dead leaves from the fall
cover the back yard.
Browning and sodden,
they plaster the grass.
Canoes are stacked against the house
and children's balls and carts
vie with the leaves, weeds
and fallen tree branches
that make this the back yard.
Hidden from the traffic
of the street and the eyes of neighbors,
dishevel of abandonment
and chaos of living
fills the back yard of the mind.

EMERGENCY ROOM

The receptionist is calm.
An old woman
is trying to vomit
behind a figured curtain.
A white wimpled nun
slides by
automatic door
closes without sound
against rubber bumpers.
Squeal of burned baby
rises to dog whistle soundlessness
behind another curtain.
Two security guards in tight Hessian blue,
pistols on hips,
walk around a supine third
who lies,
chest bare black against white bandages,
on cold chrome trolley
for x-rays.
It is 12:32 A. M.
and the doctor is explaining test results
to the ear
of a beige push-button phone.
Pain sits in straight-backed chairs,
crouches on couch cushions,
holds its guts
before ambulance entrance,
raves in a draped alcove,
waits to vanish
one way or another.

A DOG'S HISTORY

There is only pavement here.
Odors float, invisible cirrus,
from weeds in cracks
between stones or from dried urine
disappearing except to dog's scent.
No dog is naked, although
unclothed they present
buttocks to the sun
and consider genitalia
of chance acquaintances.
Without past, each writes
present with raised leg
or natural squat tickled
by grass or capricious winds.
No heaven waits perfection of dogs
but other dogs
sniffing, running, eating.

MAINE GALE
The storm comes across Casco Bay,
Thor in thunderous wrath over
some private slight, it would seem,
to the ancient Norse,
or is it the almighty Zeus,
flinging lightning flashes
to settle old scores with Apollo,
or perhaps with his ancient predecessor,
Helios, or the even earlier Persian,
Mithras , maybe Re of ancient Egypt.
The waves gallop in and crash
against the rocks raising white foam
like the manes of wild horses
ridden by ancient gods of one world
or another who cannot accept
an alternative deity's existence.
How jealous are the divinities
of their exclusive command of
the universe, land, sea, and air.

REVELATIONS

You don't know America
until you have walked The Mall.
Big butts abound, as do big bellies,
men and women alike,
young frazzled mothers with pre-school children
and no child care to secure the unleashed darlings
push the strollers and eye the Merry-Go-Round
with barely disguised lust for the coin operated respite,
while the woman at the free ear piercing booth
surrounded by racks and racks of earrings,
chats up the young guy presiding over the sunglasses center.
Deafening music pours out of the dark cavern of
Abercrombie and Fitch where the young
seek what is wicked new
in the way of garb and ornament.
Bleached blond broads with black parts splitting
their skulls stride to work in Bon Ton, the Gap,
Victoria's Secret, Penny's, the Food court
 for snacks and lunch or card games.
On a rotating pillar of a sign
an inspirational religious message circles today
behind glass where sometimes a for-profit University
hawks its wares for self-improvement
from waitress to nurse,
promising fulfillment of the American Dream
if you can get the loan
and stick it out.
It is the nightmare way.
Go into debt and leave
before you have finished
as most do.

CREATION OF THE WESTERN WORLD

We have been invented by writers.
Sophocles,
Aeschylus,
Chaucer,
Shakespeare,
Dickens,
told us who we were
and what we thought
before we knew it.
Then came Hawthorne,
Melville,
and Henry James.
Then came Hemingway,
Faulkner,
and Fitzgerald.
We grew complex,
acquired qualities
we read about,
and continued writing
and reading.
Cheever, and O'Hara,
discovered more,
followed by Updike
and Barthelme,
followed by Salinger,
Vonnegut,
and Pynchon.
Who will have the last word
or will there ever be one?
Someone will keep
creating the words

that tell us who we are
and it will always be
becoming,
rather than become.

CLEANING IT OUT

I walk through my mother's empty house.
Everywhere drawers are filled.
Bureaus are packed with satin slips
and spiced soap left behind
as trailing odor after a departing guest.
A small beaded purse filled with quarters
rests beside envelopes for future
church collection plates now past.
A worn red leather jewelry box
covered by scarves and stockings,
holds newspaper clippings of births,
deaths, weddings, a wonderful catch I made
at twelve in center field that won
baseball game and city championship.
I feel smash of ball
into sweet spot of my oiled glove
as this moment
merges with memories
for third out and everything
is now and past.
My palm stings from the impact,
but I throw the ball to the shortstop
with nonchalance
before removing the glove
to rub my hand against
my arthritic hip
in this emptying house.

ROOFERS

Bringing music and dance,
brothers, sons, cousins, nephews,
they hang flags and pennants
upon the TV antenna.
Plaid shirts at first,
in the cool of morning
for us on the ground —
they are closer to the sun —
then T-shirts, some white,
others in primary colors,
or printed with exhortations,
until the house is yacht,
adrift with coded messages.
Aloft, they rip black sheets away,
scatter sparks, marble chips, and song
as old roof is renewed.
They follow ridge pole, tight-rope
walkers balancing rolls and sheets
of black composition,
waving a roaring thrower of flame,
dragon's tongue at flick of starter.
They become dancing devils,
pirates' faces smudged
as black as the roof, filling
the hell of my heaven with more
heat covering me against
August thunder, January ice, April rain.
The one who descends to present accounts
and take my check is only my size

at my door.
Tired and hot, clothed again
in T-shirt emblazoned
NEW YORK YANKEES,
he thanks me,
smiling,
putting check in wallet worn
to conformation of human buttock.
Afterwards, nevertheless, I hear echoes
of their song and dance,
imagine Jolly Roger flying
from mast above black deck
of my ordinary house.

HEART CENTER

Waiting against the wall
in institutional chairs,
neither comfortable
nor uncomfortable,
weakened hearts in one way or another
sit within these patient
or impatient people.
Each will be called in turn
to offer a dot of life's blood
that will give up
today's character of Coumadin
coursing through veins
and arteries.
Rat poison for rodents
becomes safety net for humans.
The receptionist remains polite
but detached
and explains to some
what will happen to them.
They nod or look blank.
In turn, they are called to converse
with a welcoming nurse who reads
the numbers in a sympathetic way.
Affably she explains
diet, vegetables, drinks, pills, dosage.
Life or death seems such
an ordinary concern.

GIRL IN THE TREE

The pitch pine leans into the sea wind
and the girl perches like a tern
between branches angled against the sky.
She laughs at April danger
but clutches limbs that bend,
even under her slight form;
although she feels nearly as weightless
as if walking on the moon.
Beyond her, dunes undulate
toward the sea glimpsed
at the horizon as it is
seen through pines, bear oaks
and the sweet promise of high bush blueberries
not yet quite in bloom.
She seems to wait for something
to inform her and knows it will come.

DOGS BARK AT STRANGERS

The husky sniffs along the fence,
nose to the grass line,
his white muzzle pushes weeds
while his ice blue eyes watch
for whales in the garden.
He does not bark
at strangers to the street,
but lopes silently,
a shadow along the sh adows
of hedge and Cyclone steel links.
His legs lift and fall
without sound as if behind glass;
he circles the mowed lawn,
roses, impatiens, perennials,
muscles moving tight furred skin
over the tundra of the suburbs.
His owner puts out Gaines Burgers;
he eats, drinks, waits for silent snow.
When it comes in another season,
he lifts his head, howls.

TRUCK STOP

At the border crossing between Maine and New Hampshire,
immediately off the Interstate,
there is a truck stop selling Canadian gasoline.
Travelers stop just for the clam chowder,
whether driving a semi or a sedan.
The waitress sports a five o'clock shadow
and the ghost of a moustache.
Her smile of welcome exposes
gaps between yellow teeth.
She is hearty and loud,
a friend of all travelers
as she serves up the chowder,
and will never see fifty again.
For our tea she spills hot water
on her blue jeaned thigh
and yelps ouch ouch ouch,
that is really boiling.
She makes a joke about hot pants,
while fanning her damped crotch.
We leave her a generous tip.

WALLS

I know a man who once
put his right foot through
an inner wall of his house.
"Take this one out," he said.
Drywall powdered under his kick.
Fine dust and shreds of paper
sifted through the shaft
of sun and onto the toe
of his L. L. Bean boot.
His wife hardly seemed
to notice the demolition,
and went on simmering
her vegetable soup.
He had begun things before,
a catamaran in the back yard,
a shack in the woods,
corn rows and raspberry canes
instead of a front lawn.
She sliced nearly through
the French bread
and put it into a warm oven
to eat for lunch.
He left the holes
and the hanging remnants
of gypsum board to bring
the dog its dish.
All three ate in the sun drenching the table
with bright yellow motes of settling walls.

ANCIENTS ON THE MARCH

The ancients are on the march.
They over-run the rocks of the Galapagos,
chasing down great turtles
and the ghost of Charles Darwin.
Their cruise ships poke into fiords
as though seeking the Northwest Passage
and find souvenir shops and
name brand outlet malls.
The gulls cry and wheel overhead.
Even the holy men of the Himalayas
cannot escape as gray heads and gray beards
seek Shangri-La on the backs of Sherpas
who would probably rather drive
a Jeep Wrangler. Anyone can die
on Mount Everest if rich enough.
Professors on the loose and the take
perform for hoary alumnae
with healthy portfolios
through Greece and the Lake District.
The Great Wall of China
escapes from Kafka's pages
to come again in glossy brochures.
Crowding air terminals, train stations
and buses like 747s on wheels,
they cannot be deterred in their
missions of discovery and memories
of wasted youth in the back yard.

IMMIGRATION

Chicory time.
Stiff green shafts
shift in the wind
of autos on the roadway.
Wiry branches wave
their cornflower blue.
Blossoms daisy-like
in shape but without
the virginal white petals,
rise on these stems
to announce midsummer.
Persisting in spite of
inhospitable earth,
the seeds fallen from wagon
loads of corn,
punished under the hooves
of horses first driven by
settlers to this new land,
grow again and again.
They line the modern roads
and highways as if they belonged,
and by now they do.
Like all émigrés eventually
they have become our flowers,
as much as the daisies.
How can one tell the early
or late blossom
once the plants have settled in.

RIJKSMUSEUM AMSTERDAM

The Wardens, men and women,
look smugly out of their group portrait.
They are all satisfied in their places
and in their positions.
The appointment certifies their arrival,
Caretakers of the Lepers.
The clothing is rich and luxurious,
painted so carefully that the viewer
can almost hear the rustle of heavy fabric.
Tables hold shining utensils,
as well as gleaming goblets
whose painted surface
seem to shine like authentic glass.
Their faces shine, too, in the light
from outside the frame.
The artist captures that look of self-
importance dispensed to many
when they do good works
for the ill and deformed.
Do the subjects see the arrogance
captured there by the artist
who has been employed
to replicate nothing more than status?
Did they see the self-adulation
through the artist's eyes
or merely record the sumptuous costumes
and the grand setting
when they step back to inspect?
On the other hand, is it
all a condition of the museum visitor?

EDGE OF THE EARTH

Wild turkeys shuffle the leaves,
pecking at invisible victuals
to observers in the house.
Birds move from overturned mulch
below the underbrush and trees,
leaving behind a trail of darker brown disorder.
From beyond them,
deeper in the woods,
other birds of this flock make the sounds
of rusty hinged doors,
mythic entrances to the old world.
They hardly seem to notice one another
much less human spectators
behind reflecting window glass.
Fearless. oblivious, they scratch their way
through my tamed forest.
Curious to see if I can intrude,
I clap and whistle,
but they will not startle.
They all stare a moment
and then move on.

MONARCHS IN MAINE

Tossed in the wind with autumn leaves,
orange, black and yellow,
they taste the asters,
linger on the butter yellow golden rod,
and sample the flavor of sea gusts.
Milk weed fields welcomed them.
Now the October pods,
like miniature closed canoes ,
wait the opening days of frost.
The metamorphosis
of earth-bound bug to butterfly is complete.
Journey before them
unknown and untried,
do they fortify against
some code that requires their flight?
Does the purple of fall flowers
say that it is time,
or does the moving sun along horizon
require this pilgrimage?
We all move over the surface
of this inscrutable earth,
going and coming,
and savoring the flavor of being.

BREAKFAST AT THE MALL

It is early and the stores are still barricaded by locked iron gates.
Behind some, Lane Bryant presents
headless plus size mannequins waiting.
Under other glass, unreal playboy figures
wearing miniscule undergarments
stare in zombie seduction toward
the sexy dreams of men
locked in teenage fantasies.
The Disney store waits to clasp
in its deadly embrace
the pre-packaged frozen imaginations
of luckless children.
Everywhere there are special eternal sales,
or signs foretelling the flame-out
of some American small business vision;
although Macy's, Penny's, and Best Buy
seem everlasting like Intelligent Design.
But retail dreams are not available at 8:30 A. M.
In the middle of it all,
the food court is open
and at the tables fastened to the floor,
as if thieves in the night
might make off with the chrome and plastic
for their nefarious purposes,
senior citizens group together
over coffee and egg MacMuffins.
Gray heads, bald heads, hennaed heads
and bottle blonde heads
nod and bob as pleasantries

are created and exchanged.
It is the community of the lonely
congregating in the church of commerce
to partake of the blood and body
in a communion for left-over souls.

CALLING TO MIND

Movie titles tend to go first
along with the names of the
actors who are now much
younger than you are.
That knowledge is not
important although it
limits conversation with
art film buffs who seem
encyclopedic in their
retention of facts or data
as the current digital
world would have it.
Book titles and authors
become anonymous while
you did not notice them
slip away into the dark
of moonless nights
although you read them
just a few years ago
when they appeared on
the New York Times best
seller list in hardback
but continue to remember
the ones assigned in college
classes in your youth
and some of the immortal
lines of Shakespeare
required by teachers of
the distant past.

But the love poem
presented to that one
long lasting lover
is not forgotten since
it is rewritten each day.

FOUNDING BROTHERS

Imperfect men,
all of them,
Jefferson, Hamilton,
Adams, Franklin,
and the others less known
outside of encyclopedias.
Slave owners, land speculators,
fornicators, bastards,
murderers, and lovers
of luxury in foreign lands.
Warren G. Harding,
before Richard Nixon
our most crooked of presidents,
coined that name as he sold out
to the plutocrats in a campaign speech
after he fucked in a White House
clothes closet
and before he died in the arms
of his mistress perhaps
in a San Francisco hotel.
Even he we have glossed with the glaze of time
and he looked like a president.
But of course we do not need saints
in an official folklore.
They are simply a requirement of a mythic faith.
Only the fatuous and foolish
require that fable and its design.

COMMERCE

The crazy dog lives at the service station,
brain disconnected by gasoline fumes and coke.
Bald tires are his friends,
smelling like alley cats.
He sleeps inside one,
and absorbs odor of old rubber.
His tongue hangs out on hot days,
pink sponge full of flat soda.
He sniffs ankles of customers paying cash,
accepting a Planter's Peanut
purchased from automatic office vendor.
His love cannot be bought by peanuts.
He does not allow a scratch of the ears,
bowing his head away in charade of submission
that avoids intimacy with strangers.
Piles of empty oil cans are his Riviera
where he suns himself waiting perhaps
in twitching slumber for second coming
of canine millennium and dog heaven,
or extinction. In his lunatic world,
no moon is as bright or clear
as orange disk of Gulf insignia.

FOUND OR LOST IN QUANTUM MECHANICS

Why
is there
something
instead
of
nothing?
Will
string theory
give us
the answer?
Will
it all
matter?
What
is the
matter?
Matter
of
fact,
we wonder.

DOGS OF SAN JUAN

They would never be mistaken for wolves,
their ancestors before civilization.
Perhaps ragged coyotes.
They skulk along the street,
keeping close to buildings
as if to disappear into the stucco.
They sniff at bags left at the curb
in case there is something to eat.
Store owners wave them away
from entrances for they may discourage
customers with the unappetizing
look and smell.
Their heads hang down,
as do their tails.
Life is hard and kicks abundant
when they are noticed.
Small children who might like
to pet one are yanked away.
These are not pampered darlings,
nor do they seem to notice the live toys
carried by well-dressed ladies.
If caressed between the ears,
they respond as loved pets might,
but warily; although they are not.
In heat, bitches are mounted
in alleys by hungry canine roosters
with nothing better to do
and no one cares, or even notices,
as life is created and goes on.

They must die, but dead ones
are seldom seen for the graveyard
is hidden in some other back alley.
Americans by birth, they are never asked to
prove citizenship because
everyone knows that they belong,
if not loved or wanted.

SUPERMARKET ON THE EDGE OF CASCO BAY

The heron inspects the estuary
while mallards float into the tide
and frogs fall silent.
The parking lot edging the water
does not collapse into immobility
as shoppers wheel crammed carts
to fill the opened rear maws of SUVs
and splendid trunks of proper suburban sedans,
BMWs, Mercedes, Priuses, Audis,
and an occasional Cooper Mini,
or Honda Fit in black,
some from "away" which is the ultimate sin.
The parking is spiced with an occasional rusty
pick-up truck of some authentic Mainer
or an ancient Corolla.
Shoving aside the detritus of a genuine
lobsterman. to place the bags and boxes,
the resident shopper does not notice birds.
The heron raises its head on the long neck,
contemplating purchases not for him,
and then plunges the beak into his
natural market place for free groceries.
The mallards rise and fall on the parodies
of ocean swells that filter through the islands
to lap at the rocks below the parking lot.
They seem unconcerned with shoppers
and the heron is an alien creature to ducks
and the gallery of the supermarket.

CRESCENT BEACH IN THE MORNING

Bright colors of every kind and hue,
rainbows on the beach
in the person of small children,
active as plovers in the morning sun.
It is mostly young mothers with
infants, toddlers, and those not yet quite bloomed
into that scornful age of the teens.
They whoop, fly kites, and play games
involving patterns marked in the gray sand
and large soccer balls.
They must be locals rather than summer people,
although there are a few fathers
that mark them as tourists in season.
It all might be a circus with clowns,
but isn't, even though there is always
an extremely fat lady flopped under
a multi-colored beach umbrella,
sweating a great deal, nevertheless
and dreaming of chicken-fingers
with a double serving of fries,
or a twelve-inch Hero sandwich
with a thirty-two ounce Big Gulp.
The lobster men have taken to the sea
from Kettle Cove to check the traps.
White triangles of sails punctuate
the blue of Casco Bay,
sailing beyond the bright red kayaks
put to sea some seconds before.
Sensuality and commerce,
work and wish mingle
and that is life's combination.

MY FATHER'S OTHER WORLD

He and I did not occupy the same country.
It was the same space.
His house and land touched mine.
Grass filled the yards between
and I could not see the property line.
Cardinals called from the top of my trees.
Perwinkle spilled down my banks.
Yew, laurel, and honeysuckle spread
about the house.
Sugar maples, oaks, and hemlock
ringed the open land,
but ogres filled his forest,
dragons still breathed fire
that scorched his lawn.
Bandits waylaid travelers who turned
to his door. At night, dark forms convened
upon his steps plotting vile ceremonies.
In the morning, his eyes filled with fear
and he asked if those at our house had survived.

FORESHADOW

My daughter wrestles with her son
on the oriental rug of our living room.
He plunges his eighteen month body
across her stomach as each rolls
and laughs against patterns of red and blue
appropriate to tent and bazaar.
They hold one another
in changing embrace, warmth to warmth,
breaking free in a moment
to giggle and whoop
and clasp again in loving struggle
that is both parting and coming together.

MAN IN A BEARD

Sometimes he wears a beard and sometimes
he does not.
Wearing it, he is pirate.
Black, it bushes about his lips and chin,
turning him into Teach.
He eats a peach with abandon,
juice be-jeweling with sparkling flecks
that bestial muff about the chops.
Bear, he growls and roars,
dancing over men, women, and daughters,
terrorizing suitors for their hands,
laughing in his wine,
and building barques to sail the seven seas
under all phases of the moon,
mad as hurricanes.
Shaving,
he is revealed.
Pale cheek, paler chin,
his eyes turn sad.
He weeps.
Dogs bring him rubber balls in their teeth.
He rubs their muzzles silently,
but does not play.
Seeking counsel,
he does not sleep with his wife.
He desires neatness
and arranges his belongings
carefully along the shelves
of his existence

a place for each.
He takes up cabinetry,
building meticulous boxes out of choice woods,
concerned that corners
are mitered to perfection.
He moves into the smallest one
and closes the lid.

FLOOD

Salt water creeps over sand like a horseshoe crab,
boundary curling first over wet surface
and then edging into dry grains smoothing lumps
as if this were the usual rising tide.
Beyond lies swords of sea grass curving in Atlantic breeze,
and beyond that sparse greenery
architects' apparitions made solid come into view.
Grandiose and humble go under together,
bubbles rising to mark momentarily the spot and are gone.
Oil fields in Kuwait and Arabia anticipate water
as sun streams down through brown-white sky
turned to concentrating lens by burned oil.
Heat is held and multiplied by the stuff exhumed.
Ocean brims, pushing spindrift in white lace
along the advancing front as chunks of age-old
blue and black ice fall crashing into warming seas
thousands of miles away amongst penguins
and puffins south and north.
Range Rovers flee the Hamptons in panic
as water rolls over Land's End at Montauk.
New money is no dike, nor is old.
Mercedes head to higher ground in
flat middle eastern deserts and the mountains
of Iran and Iraq are suddenly the place to be,
despite Kurds, cold, and borders of former
colonists whose own homelands also dwindle
behind chalk cliffs and salt French flats.
San Francisco delta covers over and bridges are lower.
Refineries across the bay fizz out in rising Pacific

like burning candles sinking into a turbulent bathtub.
New Orleans vanishes in a whirlpool of floating coffins
and cars while Bourbon Street bars and tourists
spin away into the blue waters of the Gulf of Mexico.
Acid rain has filled the lakes of the Adirondacks
with clear water that is without life or future.
Go to the high hills and contemplate the sky.

MYSTERY

My father remained a detective novel without the solution.
in fiction Hercule Poirot untangles the strings of the plot
and reveals the motives and the methods of the character.
There was no Agatha Christie in life to perform that mission.
Smiling most of the time, he accepted the buffeting of
the Great Depression and its economic stresses
as he had the military demands of World War I
when he was lifted out of the tranquil and provincial Hudson
Valley
and sent to the exotic Mexican border in Texas to listen
for German spies plotting across the Rio Grande
while his young wife and my mother nursed their first child,
who was my older brother sprung on the young couple,
in the calm of small-town life beyond the reach of the big city.
Who was this pillar of the ordinary who welcomed
the customers to his country store with politeness,
gave penny candy to neighborhood children who fled
to the sanctity of the only center of the village
when thunder and lightning pounded skies and pavement
and parents were not present after school?
This father who denied panic attacks when his sons
went to another war by taking quiet restorative naps
to bring order to the terrible turmoil and turbulence within.
A private man to his children, a father who did not confide fears,
perhaps to his wife, our mother, but his children were not to know.
Manhood in his time meant presenting strength, authority,
and the self assurance that said self-reliance and confidence.
So who was to say what might have been pose or instead reality.
Would it make a difference to finally know?

TOURS

Anyone who has observed the passengers
loading one of the multi-storied tour boats
notices that the world seems awash in widows.
Some seem properly merry in the old
operatic style, and some do not.
All mount the gangplank from the mooring
garbed in the latest style for those younger
by ten to twenty years as gleaned from all
the style sources available and purchasable
from the trust funds set up by efficient mates
if now passed on, buried, or cremated,
freeing at last the wife to spend and to spend
and to hope and to hope.

GAP

At the suburban Mall
various female customers
appear grossly
obese,
walking overstuffed
furniture
desperately
seeking allure,
while the women
working
the shops,
posing like
plastic manikins
to sell that charm,
are thin as
skeletons
slip-covered
in skin.

WHY IS THERE EVIL

At seventy percent off the regular price,
you can get all the answers
from someone who knows,
or at least lectures on,
the source of evil.
One knows it is the truth
because the offer appears
on slick paper
in a widely published magazine.
We are promised THE lecture
from a renowned
Professor of Ethics
beloved by students everywhere
or so the blurb promises.
That slick paper ad
in that slick paper periodical
promises resolution
of your ETERNAL dilemma.
God?
Satan?
Humankind?
Monkey genes?
Parents?
Culture?
Educate your self
alone with your television set
or your computer monitor.
This outstanding lecturer
and academic star

shares his wisdom
with the lesser beings desperate to know.
All the SOLUTIONS on one DVD
at that attractive seventy percent off
in this special one-time only offer. Call now.
LIFE SAVING ANSWERS AWAIT YOU.

BLESSED BE

On the day celebrating
The Feast of St. Francis of Assisi
Methodists of Maine
living in Cape Elizabeth
bless the dogs.
Sharing a personal moment
with each dog,
the pastor will consecrate
the dog's life.
Following this sacred ceremony,
several contests will be held–
best dog costume
best dog trick,
dog with the longest tail,
and dog with the loudest bark.
but no dancing
or card playing —
Which god will be listening
or watching
or caring?

AGE IS AN INDIAN SUMMER

Capricious and unpredictable,
sunny and temperate one day,
gray and frosty another,
the season between seasons
has the colors of autumn
and summer mixed.
It cannot decide what to do
with what was and what will be.

COUNSEL

Take no advice.
Bite the apple yourself.
If it is sour,
throw it away.
If it is sweet,
eat it down to the core.
and remember
the variety.

THE TERRITORY AHEAD

(Built on a fragment found in a Christmas Catalogue)

"Snow is four feet deep and falling,
the SUV was buried long ago,
and the phone line is down.
You're listening to Coleman Hawkins
and reading your way through
everything that Thoreau ever wrote."
and wondering if Henry David had
driven to Walden Pond in his Hummer,
his Chevrolet Suburban, or the Range Rover ?
Did he use the taxes he refused to pay
to make the down payment
on his auto lease?
When the land lines went down,
did he turn to his cell phone for
civilized connection to Concord
and good old Ralph Waldo?
Did his simple mailbox become
crammed with fancy catalogues?
Was his sense of irony
as paralyzed as that of the purchaser
of these items of conspicuous consumption ?

MISS POTTER

was the comrade of Peter Rabbit
even if he nibbled her cabbage
and green beans as she was also
the acquaintance of Squirrel Nutkin
another inhabitant of that genuine
natural world in the Lake District
where she could roam the Fells
and cool her feet in the chilly
waters of those bodies that
gave the place its name which
woman without authority could
understand even if the male
world did not believe her important
enough to read her papers on
the character of toad stools
for if she had been Farmer MacGregor\
that would have paid attention,
but she went on to save the land
and to explain it to children who
loved her art and words because
she was a level-headed romantic
who loved the natural world
enough to preserve it in the face
of masculine despoilers and witless
pillagers who were less intelligent
than the lambs who frolicked in
the mountains calling out in their
tenor bleats more musical than
one would expect from mere beasts
but they were part of her family.

COMEDY

as people giggle and die
behind their grotesque masks
there must be some grand joke
as the gulls laugh and
sweep away the clouds
hanging over the bay
while we humans do not
get it in some natural punch line
understood only by the birds
and we observers just enjoy
the sun as it breaks through
behind the feathered friends who know
the meaning of nature while
we only know the warmth and
brightness and not the signifying

REALITY SHOW (New Verse News)
BELIEVER (New verse News)
CONTAMINATED (New Verse News)
THE LONELINESS OF THE GROCERY CART (Dead Flowers)
GHOSTLY (Broad River Review)
WHEN THE POET DIES (Galway Review)
CARDS OF IDENTIFICATION (Southern Humanities Review)
INNER SPACE (Chaffin Journal)
GRANDDAUGHTER (Timber Creek Review)
BUTTON COLLECTION
FRONT YARD PEOPLE (Timber Creek Review)
EMERGENCY ROOM (Burning Word)
A DOG'S HISTORY (Burning Word)
MAINE GALE
REVELATIONS
CREATION OF THE WESTERN WORLD
CLEANING IT OUT (Caduceus)
ROOFERS (Toyon)
HEART CENTER (Edgz)
GIRL IN THE TREE (Main Street Rag)
DOGS BARK AT STRANGERS (Green River Review)
TRUCK STOP…43(Pearl)
WALLS (White Pelican Review)
ANCIENTS ON THE MARCH (Descant)
QUESTION OF THE RIGHTEOUS (Borderlands)
RETIRED GREYHOUND (Gander Press Review)
IMMIGRATION (Galway Review)
RIJKSMUSEUM AMSTERDAM (Pennsylvania Literary Journal)
EDGE OF THE EARTH (the Aurorean)
MONARCHS IN MAINE (the Aurorean)
BREAKFAST AT THE MALL (On The Rusk)

CALLING TO MIND (Pennsylvania Literary Journal)

FOUNDING BROTHERS

COMMERCE (White Pelican Review)

FOUND OR LOST IN QUANTUM MECHANICS (*Cold Mountain Rev.*)

DOGS OF SAN JUAN

SUPERMARKET ON THE EDGE OF CASCO BAY(SMALL PRINT MAGAZINE)

CRESCENT BEACH IN THE MORNING

MY FATHER'S OTHER WORLD (Southern Humanities Review)

FORESHADOW (Futures Trading)

MAN IN A BEARD (Laurel Review)

FLOOD (Cactus Heart)

DRAMA REVEALED (Taj Mahal Review)

MYSTERY (Galway Review)

TOURS (Galway Review)

GAP (On The Rusk)

WHY IS THERE EVIL (New Verse News)

BLESSED BE (Chaffin Journal)

AGE IS AN INDIAN SUMMER (Xavier Review)

COUNSEL (Southern Humanities Review)

THE TERRITORY AHEAD (Blueline)

MISS POTTER (Taj Mahal Literary Journal)

COMEDY (Pennsylvania Literary Journal)